LEAVES

LEAVES

LINDSAY PORTER

PHOTOGRAPHS BY MICHELLE GARRETT

LORENZ BOOKS
LONDON • NEW YORK • SYDNEY • BATH

This edition published in the UK in 1997 by Lorenz Books

© 1997 Anness Publishing Limited

Lorenz Books is an imprint of
Anness Publishing Limited
Hermes House
88-89 Blackfriars Road
London SE1 8HA

This edition is published in Canada by Lorenz Books, distributed by
Raincoast Books Distribution Limited, Vancouver

The British cataloguing-in data is available from the British Library

ISBN 1 85967 337 6

Publisher: Joanna Lorenz
Introduction by: Beverley Jollands
Designer: Lilian Lindblom
Photographer: Michelle Garrett
Step photography: Lucy Tizard
Illustrator: Lucinda Ganderton

Printed in China

1 3 5 7 9 10 8 6 4 2

CONTENTS

INTRODUCTION

W hen Adam and Eve designed fig-leaf tunics for themselves they were beginning a rich and universal tradition of the use of foliage in art and craft. Thousands of different leaf forms display a natural symmetry and pattern to inspire decorative motifs: you need go no further than your own garden.

We've always used leaves in practical ways – they're basic to our existence as food and drink, and they regulate the air we breathe. In Southeast Asia, tough pandan palm leaves are still used to thatch roofs, and huge glossy banana leaves are used as wrappings for food-stuffs and as dinner plates. On Western tables, vine leaves are arranged decoratively under cheese or fruit. From using leaves as plates it's a short step to making plates like leaves: Wedgwood were producing green-glazed dishes and jugs shaped like vine and fern leaves in the 1760s. A silver-plated tea service in the shape of pitcher plants was shown at the 1851 Great Exhibition, arranged on a tray resembling the giant Victoria lily leaf, while elaborate Victorian table-centres resembled whole palm trees. But the history of leaves as a decorative motif begins far earlier.

In ancient Egypt, painted borders of stylized grasses and reeds were common. Lotus leaves were used as decoration on papyrus scrolls (which were also made of leaves), and on walls, furniture, clothes and jewellery. In the 5th century BC, Greek potters formulated ornamental motifs that spread all through the ancient world and still survive today in architecture. Among them were the acanthus leaf, which formed the capitals of columns of the Corinthian order, and the palmette, a fan-shaped leaf motif which alternated with lotus flowers to form the cornice ornament known as the anthemion. Swirling stems of leaves, particularly vine leaves, were an appropriate decoration on red and black pots which were often used to store wine.

Above: Leaves and other natural patterns have been used to decorate plates for centuries.

The vine leaf has a long history as a printer's ornament. In Venice around 1500, Aldus Manutius adapted traditional Roman designs as stamps for bookbindings, and later recut them as typographical flourishes. Used by typographers ever since as pointers or tail-pieces, these little ornaments are collectively known as "Aldine leaves".

Classical acanthus and vine leaf ornaments reached the Middle East and became part of the intricate interweaving of flat, formalized shapes that decorate Islamic buildings, textiles and pottery. A different influence on Persian pottery was Chinese art, whose more naturalistic, trailing floral and foliage motifs were much imitated in Europe. They eventually contributed to the development of Rococo, with delicate plant traceries wandering over carved wood, plasterwork and Spitalfields woven silks.

Left: This rag rug was inspired by traditional American patch-work quilt designs. Clusters of stylized oak leaves and acorns were popular, as the oak symbolized fortitude.

Indian printed textiles began to arrive in England in the later 17th century, and brought in a chunkier style of floral design. Though the Indian dyes were fast (a novelty in England), no permanent green dye was available, so that the leaves tended to fade to blue (later 19th-century chintz patterns imitated the originals by printing the leaves blue to start with). The style of patterns like the "Indian Tree", with twining stems and exotic leaves, inspired English crewel embroidery used for bed-hangings and curtains. After the Restoration of Charles II, his symbolic oak leaf was a popular embroidery motif. Later on, knitters also devised leaf stitches, such as "Falling Cable Leaf", "Sycamore", "Fern Leaves" and "Willow Buds".

The leaves with clearly identifiable outlines have acquired symbolic significance: the most sketchily drawn holly leaf conjures up Christmas, Canadians feel patriotically proud of their maple leaf, and Irish

Above: The hand-printed design on this calico curtain was inspired by the patterns typical of Indian textiles.

buttonholes sport shamrocks on St Patrick's Day. Leaves are the ancient Chinese symbols of "the Ten Thousand Things": the leaves of the Cosmic Tree represent every living thing in the universe. Chinese scholar-painters sometimes specialized entirely in paintings of bamboo, striving to achieve perfection in leaf arrangements which were given names like "flying geese" or "gathering swallows".

Above: A 19th-century band box, traditionally used for holding men's collars, decorated with an oak-leaf pattern.

Gothic architecture seems literally to sprout leaves – every feature is carved with swirling foliage. The complex fan vaulting of a cathedral roof resembles a canopy of trees, while the windows are crowned with trefoils, or clover-leaf shapes. Decorated Gothic stone-carving was brilliantly realistic: the capitals of columns were entwined with lovely swags of oak, maple, ivy, rose, hawthorn and hops. Beautiful examples of organic designs in Gothic architecture exist to this day throughout Europe.

Painters in the Gothic style used foliage as a surface decoration, with each leaf defined as clearly as in the foliage borders of an illuminated manuscript. In Botticelli's paintings the embroidered leaves on the clothes of the figures look about as real as those on the trees above them. When the artists of the Renaissance developed perspective, trees receded into the background: they became broadly defined shapes in the windless landscapes of Poussin and Claude Lorrain. When individual leaves re-emerged in painting, they were depicted as points of Impressionist light.

Above: This cupboard is decorated with the leaf and tulip designs typical of Pennsylvania Dutch patterns.

Above: Contemporary painted tiles carry on a long history of using leaf designs on friezes and borders.

Early American designers of appliquéd quilts found inspiration in their surroundings, and leaves were prominent in simple, bold patterns such as "Oak Cluster", "Cherry Trees" and "Wreath and Hearts". These were used in blocks to make symmetrical patterns and repeated as a trailing design around the edge of the piece. A single square from one of these would make an effective motif for a cushion cover. Broadly drawn leaf shapes were also used as stencils, and you can use this effective style of decoration in several of the projects in this book.

Art Nouveau drew heavily on swaying stems, curling tendrils and billowing foliage. More disciplined were the wallpapers and textiles of William Morris, who brilliantly reproduced the vigour of natural plant growth within a formal repeating pattern in popular designs like "Trellis" and "Willow", and many others still in production today.

Functionalism in interior decoration precluded ornament from the 1930s on, although if any pattern was allowed to intrude on stark room settings full of Scandinavian furniture, it could well be of leaves, as if the house plants had migrated on to the curtains. In the last few decades, when pattern and ornament have returned in a riot of chintz, embroidery, stencils and wallpapers, leaves are as prominent a motif as ever.

Above: This frieze was applied with sponges dipped in emulsion. The pattern was inspired by 19th-century American appliqué designs.

OAK-LEAF POTHOLDER

Many nineteenth-century American quilt patterns were derived from natural imagery; the flowing lines of leaves, trees and flowers were reinterpreted to create pretty symmetrical designs. This oak-leaf pattern is based on a block from an appliqué quilt made in New York State in 1850.

YOU WILL NEED

MATERIALS
fusible bonding web
green felt, 15 cm/6 in square
checked cotton fabric, 22 x 30 cm/9 x 12 in
polyester wadding, 2 x 22 cm/9 in squares
thick cotton backing fabric, 18 cm/7 in square
matching sewing thread
small eyelet screw
wooden toggle

EQUIPMENT
thin card or paper for template
fabric marker
iron
scissors
pins
sewing needle
tacking thread

1 Enlarge the template at the back of the book to measure 14 cm/5½ in across. Transfer the outline to the bonding web and iron it on to the green felt. Cut out the shape.

2 Cut a 22 cm/9 in square from the checked fabric. Peel off the backing paper from the felt square and iron centrally on to the fabric square. Press under a 1 cm /½ in hem.

3 Pin the polyester wadding squares between the backing fabric and the decorated square. Pin, tack and slip-stitch the turned edge over the backing square to conceal the raw edges.

4 For the hanger, sew together the long sides of the remaining checked fabric. Screw the eyelet into the toggle and thread the hanger through. Fold in half and sew in place.

MATISSE-INSPIRED CHILDREN'S CLOTHES

The artist Henri Matisse spent his later years creating dynamic and exciting paper collages, characterized by bold colours and strong graphic shapes. They were the inspiration behind this collection of clothes, which shows just how easy it is to customize a ready-made garment to make something really individual.

YOU WILL NEED

MATERIALS
plain white T-shirt
fusible bonding web
scraps of plain cotton fabric in
*   bright colours*
matching sewing threads
plain white long-sleeved shirt
coloured buttons
denim jacket

EQUIPMENT
thin card or paper for template
fabric marker
scissors
iron
sewing machine
sewing needle

1 Enlarge the template at the back of the book to fit your T-shirt and transfer each element of the design, in reverse, on to fusible bonding web with a fabric marker. Cut out roughly.

2 Choose three colours for the background shapes and iron one rectangle on to each. Cut out along the outline, peel off the backing paper and iron in place. Stitch around the outside edge with a narrow zigzag stitch in matching thread.

3 Cut out the branched and single leaf shapes in the same way and iron on to the shirt.

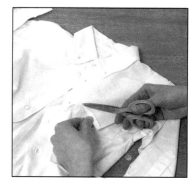

4 Sew each shape in place with zigzag stitch, working accurately around the curves. Press lightly.

5 Finish off on the reverse of the work, knotting the ends of the threads together and clipping close to the surface.

6 Customize a plain white shirt by removing the buttons and pocket. Wash and press. Sew appliqué motifs to each side of the front, as for the T-shirt.

7 Replace the white buttons with brightly coloured ones, chosen to match the appliqué.

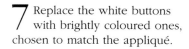

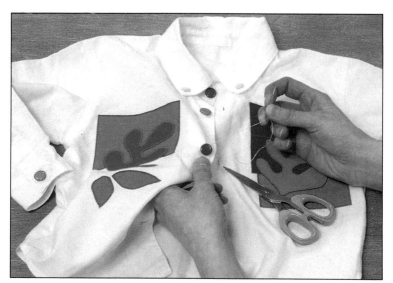

8 Decorate the back of the
denim jacket in the same
way; again, use coloured
buttons to add the final detail.

FLOATING LEAVES MOBILE

Featherlight paper leaves will flutter delicately in the merest whiff of air. Use a variety of textures for the cut-outs – look out for handmade paper incorporating leaves and flower petals.

YOU WILL NEED

MATERIALS
thick silver florist's wire
selection of coloured and
* textured papers*
matching sewing thread

EQUIPMENT
wire cutters
round-nosed pliers
thin card or paper for templates
pencil
scissors
sewing needle

1 Cut two lengths of wire 20 cm/8 in long and one length 30 cm/12 in long. Twist each piece of wire in the middle to make a loop. Make another small loop, pointing downwards, at each end of each piece.

2 Enlarge the templates at the back of the book and cut them out of thin card or paper. Draw around them on an assortment of plain and textured papers. Cut out the shapes.

3 Use a needle to attach an assortment of leaves on to a length of thread to hang from each wire loop.

4 Use thread to hang the two shorter wires from the ends of the longer one. Tie the leaves to each wire loop. Fasten a length of thread to the top loop to hang the mobile.

NEEDLEPOINT MAT

I n the 1950s leaves were a great inspiration to designers, who turned them into almost abstract shapes. The muted colours of this needlepoint are also expressive of the period.

YOU WILL NEED

MATERIALS
square of needlepoint canvas
tapestry wool: 3 shades of cream,
  2 shades of green, yellow, gold
  and black
card
black velvet for backing
PVA glue

EQUIPMENT
sewing needle
tacking thread
waterproof marker pen
tapestry needle
scissors
ruler
craft knife
cutting mat

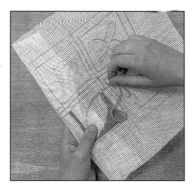

1 Tack vertically and horizontally across the canvas to mark the centre. Mark the design on the canvas. Following the chart at the back of the book, in which each square represents a stitch, work the pattern in half cross stitch.

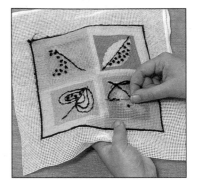

2 When the half cross stitch is complete, thread the needle with black wool and embroider the details. Work the straight lines in back stitch and use French knots for the dots.

3 Measure the needlepoint and cut a piece of card to the same size. Cut out a piece of velvet to this size plus 2 cm/¾ in turning allowance all round. Spread glue on the card and stick it centrally on to the back of the velvet. Clip the corners, fold over the turning allowance and glue in place. Trim the canvas and clip the corners; turn the allowance to the wrong side. Spread glue on the wrong side of the card and press the needlepoint in place.

ITALIANATE TILES

These Florentine-style tiles are based on ceramic decoration of the Renaissance. They are painted with easy-to-use enamel paints which are fixed in the oven. A single tile could be a focal point in a bathroom, but when several are arranged together, interesting repeat patterns are formed. Adapt the colours to fit in with your own decor.

YOU WILL NEED

MATERIALS
plain white square tiles
ceramic enamel paints:
  mid-green, dark blue-green,
  rust-red and dark blue

EQUIPMENT
tracing paper
soft pencil
sticky tape
hard pencil
medium and fine paintbrushes
paint-mixing container

1 Wash and dry the tiles thoroughly. Enlarge the template at the back of the book to fit the size of your tiles. Trace off the main motif (and the border if you wish) and rub over the back of the tracing with a soft pencil. Position the tracing on each tile, secure with tape, and draw over the outline with a hard pencil.

2 Paint the leaf in mid-green enamel paint and allow to dry. You may need to mix colours to achieve the shades you wish. Using a dark blue-green, paint over the outline and mark in the veins. Paint a dot in each corner of the tile in the same colour.

3 With a fine brush, paint a border of rust-coloured leaves and a slightly larger leaf in each corner. Paint a curved scroll to either side of the large leaf in dark blue. Repeat with the remaining tiles. When the paint is completely dry, fix in the oven according to the manufacturer's instructions.

LEAF BOX

Keep this sturdy little box on your desk to hold bits and pieces, or make it to hold a memorable gift for someone special.

YOU WILL NEED

MATERIALS
8 x 45 mm/³⁄₈ x 1¾ in
  pine slat
wood glue
4 mm/¼ in birch-faced
  plywood sheet
white undercoat paint
acrylic paints: bright yellow and
  dark and light green
clear gloss acrylic varnish

EQUIPMENT
ruler
fretsaw
sandpaper
masking tape
pencil
medium and fine paintbrushes
paint-mixing container

1 Cut four equal lengths of pine slat and sand the rough edges. Glue together to form the sides of the box, holding in place with masking tape. Draw a leaf shape freehand on to plywood. Cut out and sand.

2 Draw around the inside and outside of the box on to the plywood for the lid insert, lid and base. Cut out and sand. Glue in the base. Sand the insert to fit and glue to the lid. Sand all around the box.

3 Paint the box and leaf shape with two coats of undercoat. Sand between coats. When dry, draw the triangles and border on the sides and lid.

4 Paint the box yellow and the border and triangles green. Finish with a coat of gloss varnish. Paint the leaf and varnish. Glue the leaf to the lid.

IVY-LEAF STOOL

This delicately painted little seat would look charming in the leafy surroundings of a garden room or conservatory.

YOU WILL NEED

MATERIALS
wooden stool
white emulsion paint
acrylic paints: sap-green
  and white
clear gloss acrylic varnish

EQUIPMENT
sandpaper
medium and fine paintbrushes
paper for template
acetate sheet
masking tape
permanent marker pen
craft knife
cutting mat
stencil brush
paint-mixing container

1 Sand the stool and paint with two or three coats of white emulsion paint. Enlarge the template at the back of the book. Tape the acetate over the design and draw the outlines of the leaves with a permanent marker pen.

3 Using sap-green acrylic paint mixed with a little white, stencil the leaves all over the stool. Allow to dry.

2 Cut out the stencil carefully using a craft knife.

4 Using sap-green acrylic paint and a fine brush, paint the tendrils, outlines and veining on the leaves. Finally, protect the stool with two or three coats of gloss varnish.

TRAILING LEAVES STORAGE TINS

Cheer up a set of simple metal containers to give your kitchen shelves a bright new look. The tins are painted with a stipple technique which gives a textured, sponged effect.

YOU WILL NEED

MATERIALS
2 metal storage tins
white matt spray paint
acrylic paints: yellow, green,
  rust-brown, dark brown
  and blue
matt spray varnish

EQUIPMENT
soft pencil
medium and fine paintbrushes
paint-mixing container
tracing paper for template
hard pencil

1 Wash the tins and lids. Spray with several coats of white paint. Mark wavy lines at the top and bottom of each tin. Fill in either side of the lines with yellow and green paint. Use a dry brush and a stippling action, adding some areas of darker colour. You may need to mix colours to achieve the shades you wish.

2 Enlarge the leaf band pattern at the back of the book. Transfer it to the central panel with tracing paper and soft and hard pencils, adding extra sections of the design so that it fits all the way round. Paint the large trefoil leaves green and the small leaves rust-brown.

3 Paint a dark brown band on either side of the leaf panel. Add a few blue dots in the spaces. Outline the leaves with darker shades of brown and green, then paint the tendrils brown. Paint the main part of the lid green, picking out the details in brown and blue. Finish off by spraying with a protective matt varnish.

LEAFY PICTURE FRAMES

The stylish raised leaf patterns around these frames are simple to create using ordinary white interior filler instead of paint to fill in the stencilled shapes.

YOU WILL NEED

MATERIALS
2 wooden frames
dark green acrylic paint
ready-mixed interior filler

EQUIPMENT
medium paintbrush
fine-grade sandpaper
thin card or paper for templates
pencil
stencil card
scissors
stencil brush

1 Paint the frames dark green. When dry, gently rub them down with sandpaper to create a subtle distressed effect.

2 Enlarge the templates at the back of the book to fit the frames. Transfer the designs to stencil card and cut them out.

3 Position a stencil on the first frame and stipple ready-mixed filler through the stencil. Reposition the stencil and continue all round the frame. Leave to dry.

4 Repeat with a different combination of motifs on the second frame. When the filler is completely hard, gently smooth the leaves with fine-grade sandpaper.

FOREST THROW

This appliqué throw recycles an old blanket as its background fabric and is pleasingly quick to put together, using fusible bonding web. Old buttons and bold woollen embroidery stitches add detail and colour.

MATERIALS
cream blanket
matching and contrasting
  crewel wool
four pieces of flannel fabric,
  each 25cm x 50 cm/10 x 20 in
felt squares in green, rust and
  brown, 30 cm/12 in
fusible bonding web,
  1.5 m/1½ yd
assorted shirt buttons (optional)
65 larger brown buttons
  (optional)

EQUIPMENT
tape measure
scissors
tapestry needle
thin card or paper for templates
fabric marker
iron
pressing cloth

1 Cut a rectangle measuring 1 x 1.3 m/40 x 50 in from the blanket. Fold under a 1.5 cm/½ in hem around the outside edge and sew with a large blanket stitch worked in cream wool.

2 Enlarge the diamond template at the back of the book so that it measures 20 cm/8 in high and use this as a guide for cutting out 25 diamonds of different colours from the flannel fabric.

3 Enlarge the leaf templates to fit within the diamonds. For each motif, choose a felt colour that will tone with the background fabric. Trace the various leaf outlines, in reverse, on to fusible bonding web with a fabric marker. Cut out roughly and iron on to the felt, then cut out neatly. Peel off the backing paper and iron a leaf to the centre of each diamond.

4 Sew the leaves down using a single strand of crewel wool and a running stitch or blanket stitch – follow the picture as a guide. Some of the leaves have an extra appliquéd motif or a cut-out shape; you can make your own variations on these ideas.

5 Use straight stitch to embroider a vein pattern on some leaves and sew on the extra motifs with cross or straight stitches.

6 Sew on tiny shirt buttons as a finishing touch, or add embroidered stars. (If the throw is for a small child, do not use buttons.) Each leaf can be different, or you could make several in the same colours.

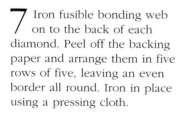

7 Iron fusible bonding web on to the back of each diamond. Peel off the backing paper and arrange them in five rows of five, leaving an even border all round. Iron in place using a pressing cloth.

8 If desired, sew a large
button over each diamond
intersection, using wool in a
contrasting colour.

GARDEN APRON

For this project you may need access to a colour photocopier. A collection of prints of old botanical paintings would make a beautiful apron for a horticulturally minded friend.

YOU WILL NEED

MATERIALS
*selection of colour images
  of leaves*
cotton apron

EQUIPMENT
scissors
masking tape (optional)
image transfer gel
medium paintbrush
soft cloth

1 Make a selection of images and photocopy them in colour if you want to create a repeat pattern.

2 Cut around each leaf shape until you have enough to cover the apron.

3 Plan your design by positioning the leaves on the apron, face down. Secure them with masking tape if required. Paint a thick layer of transfer gel on to the first motif. Replace the image face down on the apron and rub with a soft cloth. Repeat with all the images and leave to transfer overnight. Soak the cloth with clean water and rub away the paper. The images will have transferred to the fabric.

LEAF MOTIF ESPRESSO CUP & SAUCER

Browsing around antique stalls, you sometimes come across coffee cups hand-painted with broad brush strokes and lots of little raised dots of paint. It is simple to decorate your own coffee service in this style.

YOU WILL NEED

MATERIALS
white ceramic cup and saucer
green acrylic ceramic paint
pewter acrylic paint with
  nozzle-tipped tube

EQUIPMENT
acetone or other grease-
  dispersing alcohol
cotton buds
pencil
thin card or paper for templates
scissors
sticky-backed plastic
medium paintbrush
hair dryer (optional)
craft knife

1 Clean any grease from the surface of the china to be painted, using the acetone and a cotton bud.

2 Draw leaves and circles freehand on to thin card or paper. Cut them out and draw around them on the backing of the sticky-backed plastic. Cut out. Peel away the backing paper and stick the pieces in position on the cup and saucer.

3 Paint around the shapes with the ceramic paint, applying several coats to achieve a solid colour. Leave each coat to air-dry or use a hair dryer for speed.

4 To ensure a clean edge, cut around each sticky shape with a craft knife, then peel off.

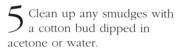

5 Clean up any smudges with a cotton bud dipped in acetone or water.

6 Using pewter paint and the nozzle-tipped paint tube, mark the outlines and details of the leaves with rows of small dots. Leave to air-dry for 36 hours. Bake the cup and saucer in the oven, following the manufacturer's instructions. The paint will withstand everyday use and gentle washing up, but not the dishwasher.

WOODLAND GIFT-WRAP

Look out for interestingly textured card and paper in complementary colours to make a whole range of greetings cards, postcards, gift wrap and gift tags for beautiful Christmas or birthday gifts.

YOU WILL NEED

MATERIALS
selection of coloured and
  textured papers and card
PVA glue
selection of acrylic paints
narrow paper ribbon
sealing wax
fresh leaves

EQUIPMENT
thin card or paper for templates
pencil
scissors
craft knife
cutting mat
ruler
stencil card
cotton wool or stencil brush
paint-mixing container
hole punch
safety matches

1 Enlarge the leaf templates at the back of the book on to thin card or paper and cut them out. Cut a rectangle of coloured card and fold it in half to make a greetings card. Draw around a leaf template on the front and cut out the shape with a craft knife. Cut a contrasting paper to the same size as the card and stick it on the inside.

2 Fold a second card, and draw around the template of the oak leaf on the reverse of the corrugated paper. Cut out the shape and glue it to the front of the card.

3 For the stencilled card, tear a square of coloured paper and glue it to the front of a piece of card. Draw around a leaf template on to stencil card and cut it out with a craft knife. Place the stencil on the coloured square and dab paint on to it with a ball of cotton wool or a stencil brush.

4 Use the same stencil on a large sheet of coloured paper to make co-ordinating gift-wrap.

5 Make a selection of gift tags and postcards in the same way. Cut some leaf shapes out of coloured paper to make simple tags. Punch a hole in the tags and thread with ribbon.

6 Make your own simple envelopes by folding a piece of coloured paper to fit around a greetings card. Secure the flaps with sealing wax and decorate while it is still sticky with a small fresh leaf.

PAINTED ORGANZA SCARF

Use muted, autumnal colours for this delicate, sheer scarf. The painted and embroidered leaves create an almost abstract pattern.

YOU WILL NEED

MATERIALS
silk organza or chiffon
fabric paints: green and blue
machine embroidery thread:
* orange and red*
matching sewing thread

EQUIPMENT
embroidery hoop
fine paintbrush
paint-mixing container
iron
sewing machine with
* darning foot*
scissors
sewing needle

1 Wash the silk to remove any dressing. Stretch the fabric taut in an embroidery hoop. Paint the leaf shapes freehand in greens and blues, mixing the paints to achieve subtle shades. Make sure the paint is dry before moving the hoop along the fabric. Iron the silk to fix the paint, following the manufacturer's instructions.

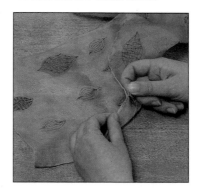

2 Select the darning- or free-stitch mode on the sewing machine and attach a darning foot. With the silk in an embroidery hoop, stitch the details in orange and red thread over the painted leaves.

3 Trim and roll the raw edges of the scarf and slip stitch the hems in place.

GARLAND TRAY

The simple leaf design for this pretty découpage tray is folded and cut out like a row of dancing paper dolls: make sure when drawing the design that your outline continues to the folds so that your paper garland will stay in one piece when it is opened out.

YOU WILL NEED

MATERIALS
wooden tray
yellow emulsion paint
large sheet of green paper
PVA glue
clear gloss acrylic varnish

EQUIPMENT
medium paintbrushes
pencil
scissors
scrap paper

1 Paint the tray with two coats of yellow emulsion paint and allow to dry. Place the tray on the green paper and draw around it. Cut out the shape just inside the line.

2 Fold the paper in half, then in half again. Draw a series of connecting leaf shapes on to scrap paper and cut out. When you are happy with the design, draw around it on to the green paper, making sure that it reaches the folded edges. Cut along the pencil line.

3 Open out the garland carefully and glue it on to the tray. Leave to dry.

4 Protect the tray with up to four coats of varnish.

LEAFY PENCIL POT

This useful pencil pot is stencilled with a simple leaf motif over a dark green background painted with a "dragged" effect.

YOU WILL NEED

MATERIALS
8 x 45 mm/³⁄₈ x 1¾ in pine slat
8 x 70 mm/³⁄₈ x 2¾ in pine slat
wood glue
white undercoat paint
acrylic paints: green, blue
* and yellow*
PVA glue

EQUIPMENT
ruler
fretsaw
masking tape
sandpaper
medium paintbrushes
stencil card
craft knife
cutting mat
pencil
paint-mixing container

1 Cut two 9 cm/3½ in lengths of each pine slat. Glue with wood glue to form the sides of the pot. Hold with masking tape until the glue is dry.

2 Sand all rough edges. Measure the inside dimensions of the pot and cut a piece of wood to make the base. Glue it in place and leave to dry.

3 Paint with two coats of white undercoat, sanding lightly between coats. Cut a piece of stencil card the same size as the broad side of the pot. Draw a leaf design and cut out with a craft knife.

4 Mix the paints to achieve blue-green and yellow-green. Apply blue-green paint with a stiff brush to show the brush strokes. Stencil the leaf pattern in yellow-green. Finish with a coat of diluted PVA glue.

DECOUPAGE OAK-LEAF BOX

Find one pretty motif and you can create lovely repeat patterns with it instantly, using a photo-copier. Copies of old engravings are perfect for this technique: here they were delicately hand-coloured in autumnal shades.

YOU WILL NEED

MATERIALS
wooden box
cream emulsion paint
black and white leaf motif
acrylic paints: yellow-ochre and
  red oxide
PVA glue
clear gloss acrylic varnish

EQUIPMENT
medium and fine paintbrushes
paint-mixing container
scissors
craft knife
cutting mat

1 Paint the box with two or three coats of cream emulsion paint. Make copies of the leaf motif in two sizes for the sides and lid. Hand-tint the copies with a thin wash of yellow-ochre, then red oxide.

2 Use scissors to cut around the outside of the leaf shapes. Cut away any small spaces within the design with a craft knife.

3 Arrange the leaves on the lid and sides of the box. Glue them on with PVA glue and leave to dry.

4 Protect the box with two or three coats of gloss varnish.

SPARKLING IVY GARLAND

Make this beautiful jewelled crown of leaves for a midsummer night's party, or perhaps for a summer wedding.

YOU WILL NEED

MATERIALS
fine green wool or green
  stranded embroidery thread
metallic threads: silver and
  blended gold and silver
sewing threads: dark and
  light green
fine silver or brass wire:
  0.6 mm for circlet,
  0.4 or 0.2 mm for leaves
selection of beads

EQUIPMENT
water-soluble fabric
embroidery hoop
paper or thin card for template
fabric marker
large-eyed needle
sewing machine with
  size 11 needle
scissors
kitchen paper

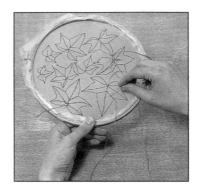

1 Stretch the water-soluble fabric on to the embroidery hoop. Enlarge the template from the back of the book and trace on to the fabric using a fabric marker. There are two styles of leaf: the first is mainly metallic; the second is overlaid with cotton thread. For the first style, hand-sew the central veins of the leaves in fine green wool or stranded embroidery thread. Use a running stitch, and use thicker thread for the larger leaves.

2 For the second style of leaf, work the veins and outlines on the machine with a straight stitch, using silver metallic thread in the bobbin and dark green sewing thread in the needle. Fill in between the veins with the lighter green. For the first style of leaf, fill in with blended gold and silver thread in the bobbin and silver thread in the needle.

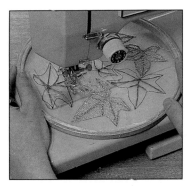

3 Sew randomly across the machined lines within each section of leaf to make the tiny veins (this also holds the embroidery together).

4 Work a zigzag stitch up the central veins and around the outer edge of each leaf to stiffen it.

5 Cut the leaves off the hoop and dissolve the fabric of each one in turn in water. Pat dry on kitchen paper. While each leaf is still damp, fold it in half and press with your fingers to make a naturalistic crease along the central vein. Open out and leave to dry.

6 Continue to embroider more leaves in both styles to make enough for the whole garland. Sew each leaf on to fine wire.

7 Twist a piece of thicker wire into a band to fit your head. Twist on more wire to make loops for attaching the leaves. Make the loops higher at the front of the garland.

8 Wind the wired leaves on to the loops on the band, using the larger leaves at the front. Add beads threaded with more wire. Bend and arrange the leaves into shape.

FROSTED FLOWER VASE

This is a magical way to transform a plain glass vase into something stylish and utterly original. Check the vase all over to make sure that it is evenly frosted before you peel off the leaf shapes: it may be necessary to paint on another coat of etching cream.

YOU WILL NEED

MATERIALS
coloured glass vase

EQUIPMENT
thin card or paper for templates
pencil
scissors
sticky-backed plastic
etching cream
medium paintbrush

1 Wash and dry the vase. Enlarge the templates at the back of the book on to thin card or paper. Cut them out. Draw around the templates on to the backing of the plastic and draw small circles freehand.

2 Cut out the shapes and peel off the backing paper. Arrange the shapes all over the vase. Smooth them down carefully to avoid any wrinkles.

3 Paint the etching cream over the vase and leave it in a warm place to dry, following the manufacturer's instructions.

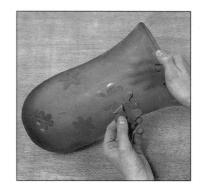

4 Wash the vase in warm water to remove the cream. If the frosting looks smooth, you can remove the shapes. If not, repeat with another coat of etching cream, then wash and remove the shapes.

STENCILLED SPRIG CURTAIN

The regular repeat pattern is easy to achieve by ironing the curtain fabric to mark a grid before you start to stencil. Alternatively, the leaf motif could be stencilled randomly across the fabric for a more informal look. Wash and iron the fabric before you start.

YOU WILL NEED

MATERIALS
cotton voile to fit window
stencil fabric paints: green, blue, brown and pink
matching sewing thread
curtain wire

EQUIPMENT
thin card or paper for template
pencil
stencil card
craft knife
cutting mat
iron
newspaper
masking tape
spray adhesive
thick and thin stencil brushes
paint-mixing container
sewing machine

1 Enlarge the template at the back of the book so that it is 17 cm/6½ in high. Transfer the outline to stencil card and cut out with a craft knife. Fold the fabric into 20 cm/8 in vertical pleats and 25 cm/10 in horizontal pleats, then press lightly to leave a grid pattern. Cover your work surface with newspaper and tape the fabric down so that it is fairly taut.

2 Spray the back of the stencil with adhesive and place it in the first rectangle. Mix the paints to achieve subtle shades. Paint the leaves in green, adding blue at the edges for depth. Paint the stem in brown and the berries in a brownish pink. Repeat in alternate rectangles.

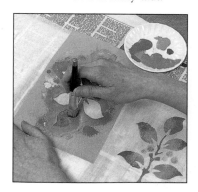

3 Turn the stencil upside-down and, with pink, paint the top leaf in the centre of the plain rectangles. Add a darker shade at the tip and mark the stalk in brown. When complete, fix the fabric paints according to the manufacturer's instructions. Hem the sides and lower edge of the curtain. Make a 2.5 cm/ 1 in channel at the top and insert the curtain wire.

TEMPLATES

To enlarge the templates to the correct size, use either a grid system or a photocopier. For the grid system, trace the template and draw a grid of evenly spaced squares over your tracing. To scale up, draw a larger grid on to another piece of paper. Copy the outline on to the second grid by taking each square individually and drawing the relevant part of the outline in the larger square. Finally, draw over the lines to make sure they are continuous.

Oak-leaf Potholder, p12

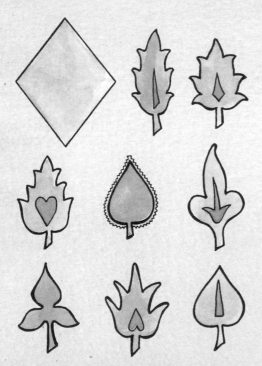

Forest Throw, p32

Ivy-leaf Stool, p26

Needlepoint Mat, p20

Italianate Tiles, p22

Floating Leaves Mobile, p18
Leafy Picture Frames, p30
Woodland Gift-wrap, p41
Frosted Flower Vase, p56

Sparkling Ivy Garland, p52

Trailing Leaves Storage Tins, p28

Stencilled Sprig Curtain, p58

Matisse-inspired Children's Clothes, p14

Acknowledgements

The author and publishers would like to thank the following people for designing the projects in this book:

Petra Boase

Floating Leaves Mobile pp18–19;
Leafy Picture Frames pp30–31;
Garden Apron pp36–37;
Woodland Gift-wrap pp41–43;
Frosted Flower Vase pp56–57

Louise Brownlow

Sparkling Ivy Garland pp52–55

Lucinda Ganderton

Oak-leaf Potholder pp12–13;
Matisse-inspired Children's Clothes pp14–17;
Italianate Tiles pp22–23;
Trailing Leaves Storage Tins pp28–29;
Forest Throw pp32–35;
Stencilled Sprig Curtain pp58–59

Jill Hancock

Leaf Box pp24–25;
Leafy Pencil Pot pp48–49

Isabel Stanley

Needlepoint Mat pp20–21;
Leaf Motif Espresso Cup & Saucer pp38–40;
Painted Organza Scarf pp44–45

Emma Whitfield

Garland Tray pp46–47

Josephine Whitfield

Ivy-leaf Stool pp26–27
Découpage Oak-leaf Box pp50–51

Picture Credits
Debbie Patterson: p8 top, p11 top
Graham Rae: p9, p11 bottom
Steve Tanner: p8 bottom, p10